Martha Washington

Her first few days as First Lady

Author Barbie Marie
Barbara Schlichting
Illustrated by Terry Honstead

Dedicated to the First Ladies
© 2018
Publisher First lady Press
ISBN 978-0-9995630-5-2

Books by Barbie Marie:
Red Shoes

Books published by Darkhouse Books:
Dolley Madisen: Blood Spangled Banner
Mary Lincoln: If Words Could Kill
Edit Roosevelt: The Clue of the Dancing Bells

Books published by First Lady Press:
Body on the Tracks

Poetry:
Whispers From the Wind

Martha Washington

Her first few days as First Lady

In 1789, on a Wednesday, First Lady Martha Washington's carriage driver stopped in front of the leased Samuel Osgood house on the corner of Cherry and Dover Street in New York City. The East River was three blocks away. The streets were very busy with carriages, animals, and street vendors because the arrival of ships on the riverfront. Crowds of people followed her brigade to the Presidential house to catch a glimpse of the president's wife.

"We've arrived ," Mrs. Washington said to her adopted two grandchildren, Nelly and Wash. (Short for Washington). "Let's see our new home." Mrs. Washington was thrilled to meet her new servants and tour her new home. "Shall we, children?"

    The driver opened the carriage door and they stepped out onto the street. Servants from inside of the house hurried to greet her.

    Itty, a young servant girl, rushed to greet the First Lady. Me, Gloria, a ragdoll, rode in Itty's pocket. (Unbeknownst to Itty, Gloria understood everything that was said, and she told stories to her doll friends in the evening when the household was asleep).

Through my eyes, Mrs. Washington looked nice and friendly. She was short and plump, with a twinkle in her eye. President Washington was delighted to see her. The couple was complete opposite in size and shape, but when he leaned over and whispered in her ear, she giggled.
I knew this Mrs. Washington would be nice.

"What a lovely home, George," Mrs. Washington said, entering. "It's a fine brick building and a 'handsomely furnished house'."

First Lady Mrs. Washington barely had time to greet her husband because of the throngs of people who followed her inside.

"I will have another servant take the children to the nursery," Oney Judge said. She spoke to the woman.
"Nelly and Wash, come with me." It wasn't long before the children were led into the nursery.

In the morning, Itty gave me a bright smile and hid me inside of her apron pocket. "Don't tell anyone you're in here, Gloria, I don't want to get into trouble."

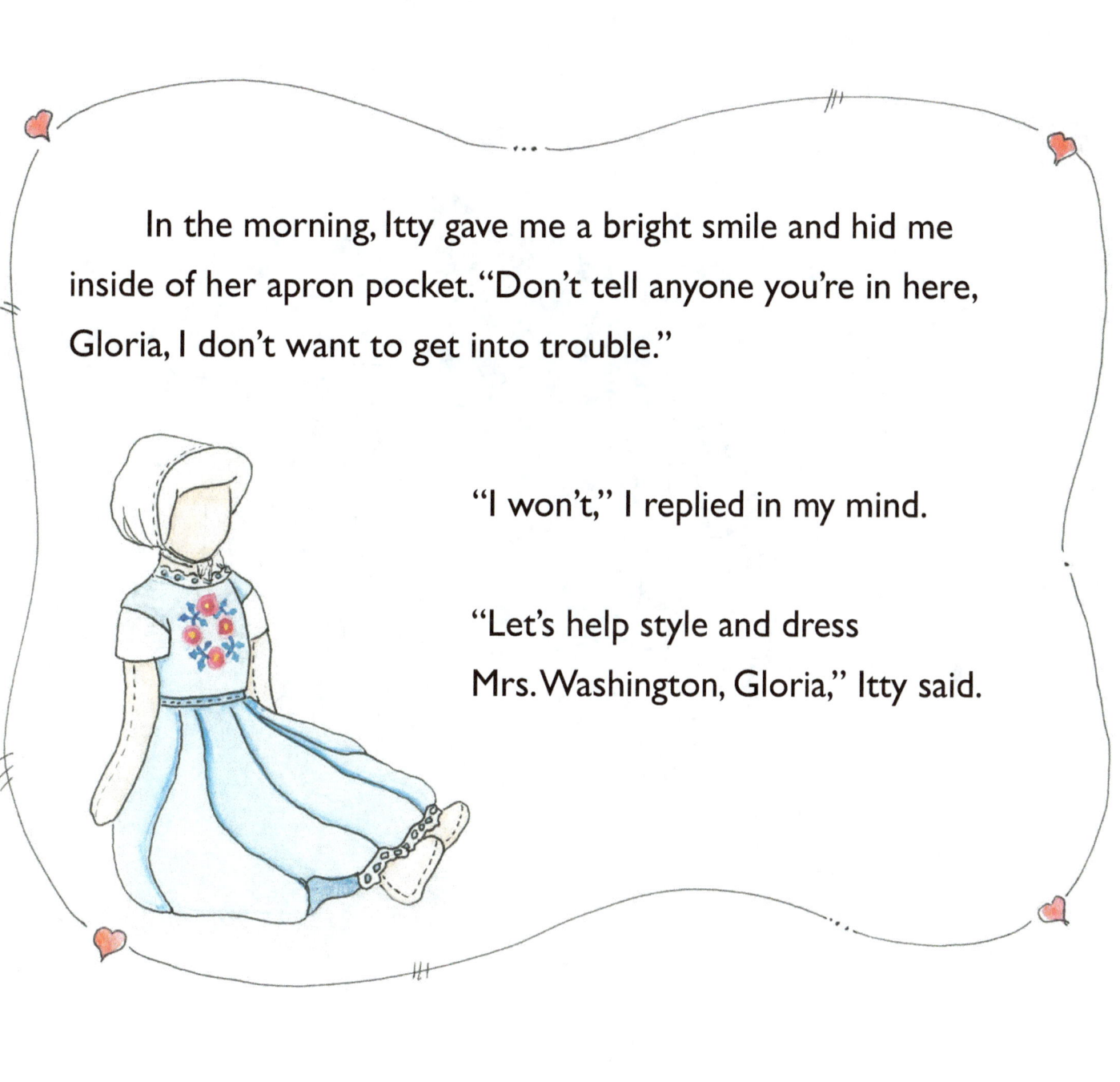

"I won't," I replied in my mind.

"Let's help style and dress Mrs. Washington, Gloria," Itty said.

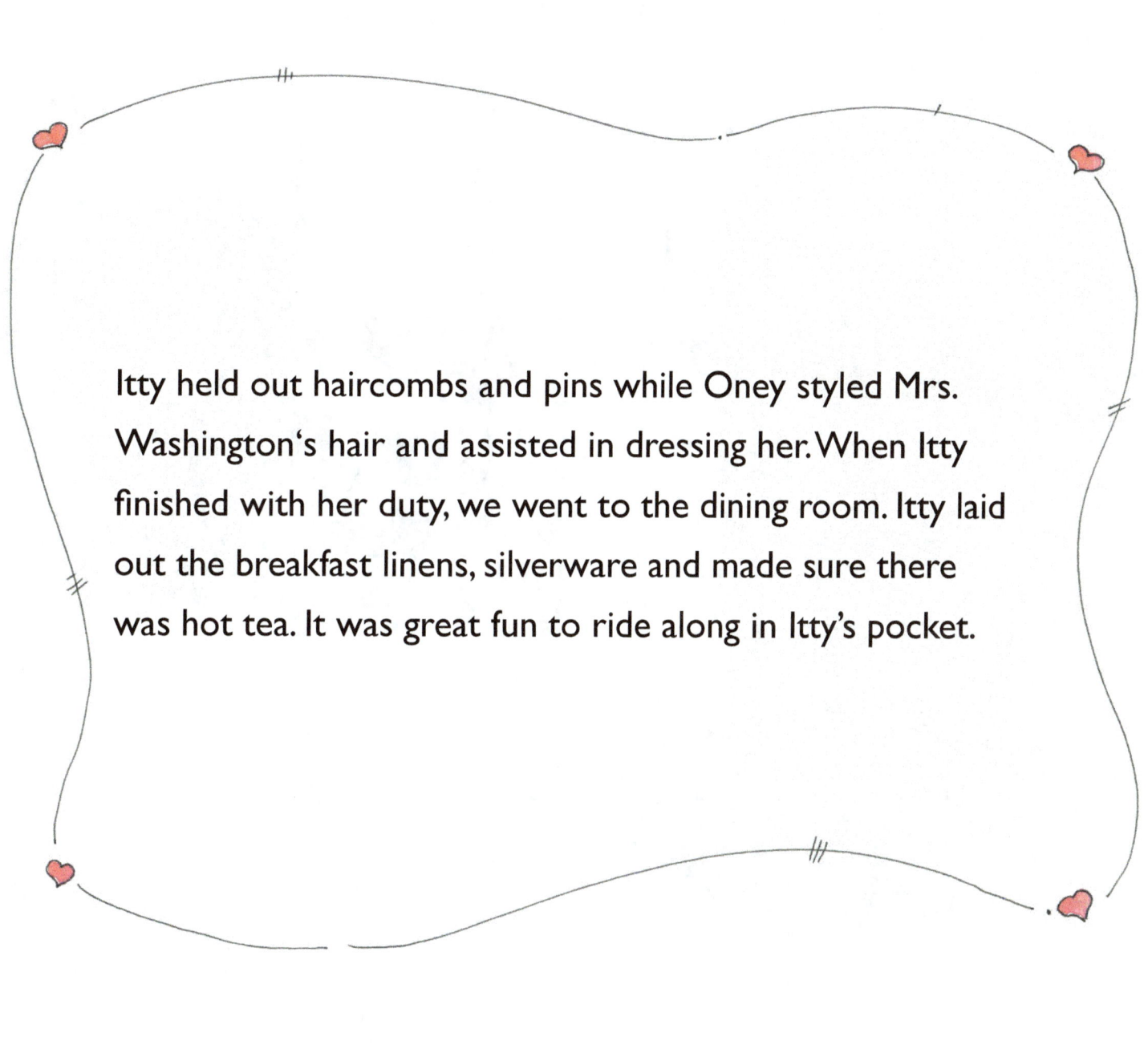

Itty held out haircombs and pins while Oney styled Mrs. Washington's hair and assisted in dressing her. When Itty finished with her duty, we went to the dining room. Itty laid out the breakfast linens, silverware and made sure there was hot tea. It was great fun to ride along in Itty's pocket.

From Thursday morning on, I was always tucked inside of Itty's pocket. It made me accessible to all matters concerning Mrs. Washington. Mrs. Washington barely had time to settle in because of all the well-wishers who came to meet her and the president.

Itty didn't have her ears covered so I didn't either. We heard President and Mrs. Washington discuss the role of a First Lady.

"Why am I not allowed to invite my friends for tea or sewing?" Mrs. Washington asked.

"We can not show favoritism. Thursday evening's we will host dinner parties. The guest list will be politically balanced and invited by the party," Mr. Washington said.

"What else do I need to know?"

"Friday evening, beginning tomorrow night, you will host a reception. When Congress is in session, you will accept acquaintances into the house."

"When will I be allowed to invite and have tea with my friends?"

"Only certain individuals are invited here. We must be non-partisan."

Itty stood when her lady left the room and entered the hallway.

"Gloria , let's watch her," Itty said.

"She looks sad," I said in my mind.

Lady Washington held her head down and didn't look up until sitting by her writing desk in the study. She wiped her nose and wore a little smile instead of her normal big one.

Mrs. Washington asked for tea. Itty placed me near a pillow where I observed my lady. After catching up on correspondence, she reached for her knitting bag. She knit warm woolen socks.

"Here is your tea," Itty said. She set the tray with tea and biscuits down. "Who are the socks for?"

"There are plenty of people in need after the war," Mrs. Washington replied.

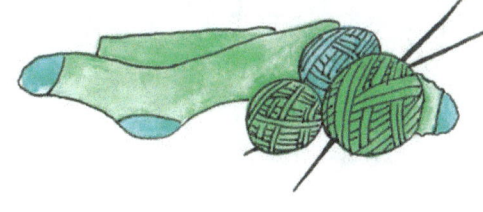

On Friday, the household bustled with guests. Mrs. Washington barely had a moment before she had to get ready for the evening's reception.

"Tonight is my first reception," Mrs. Washington said. "Itty, will you make sure that the children are entertained? I fear it'll be a long evening."

"Yes Mrs. Washington," Itty said.

Before guests arrived, Itty placed me in a back corner of the drawing room so I could watch and listen. Mrs. Washington received both women and men as long as they were dressed formally. They discussed politics of the day.

After the evening emptied of guests, Itty came for me. She helped Mrs. Washington undress and comb out her hair. She dropped a comb, but I wasn't able to pick it up and give it to her.

The following morning, Itty placed me near Mrs. Washington in her private quarters. At that very moment when I thought she was tired, she yawned and wiped her eyes. It wasn't long before the children disrupted her quiet thoughts for an early morning display of affection. Once they were out the door, Mrs. Washington picked up her quilt square from a basket and began studying it. I noticed that she'd painstakingly cut blocks to a certain measurement. She held one up high for me to see.

Suddenly, she winked and smiled at me! Just as quick, she tapped my nose!

I watched with reverence from that moment on as she pieced together the rose quilt block. When morning sewing time came to a close, she was summoned to entertain more unknown guests. I was picked up by Mrs. Washington and carried me along.

Everyday was filled with guests entering the house without invitations. The week flew by and soon it was the following Thursday when they hosted a formal dinner party.

Itty placed me high up on a cabinet in the dining room. Music announced President Washington entrance. I watched the guests and the President and First Lady sit.

"Good evening, Mrs. Adams," Mrs. Washington told the lady beside her.

"I am the Vice-Presidents wife. Call me Abigail. What is the song title?"

"The President's March and its played every time he enters a room."

Conversation flowed and the evening came to an end. Itty came for me and tucked me once again inside of a pocket.

Itty turned back the covers of the canopied bed with curtains because it kept the heat in. The bed was fashionably long for Mr. Washington.

I was whisked away by one of Abigail Adams' grandchildren. I wondered what would become of me?

Gloria—the wandering ragdoll.

First Lady Martha Washington supported her husband until he resigned from his second term in office. Both looked forward to retirement from public life.

The capital in Philadelphia was better to her liking because it was his second term. As First Lady, she was allowed to choose her guests and had more control over official dinners and receptions.

www.ingramcontent.com/pod-product-compliance
Lightning Source LLC
Chambersburg PA
CBHW060428010526
44118CB00017B/2413